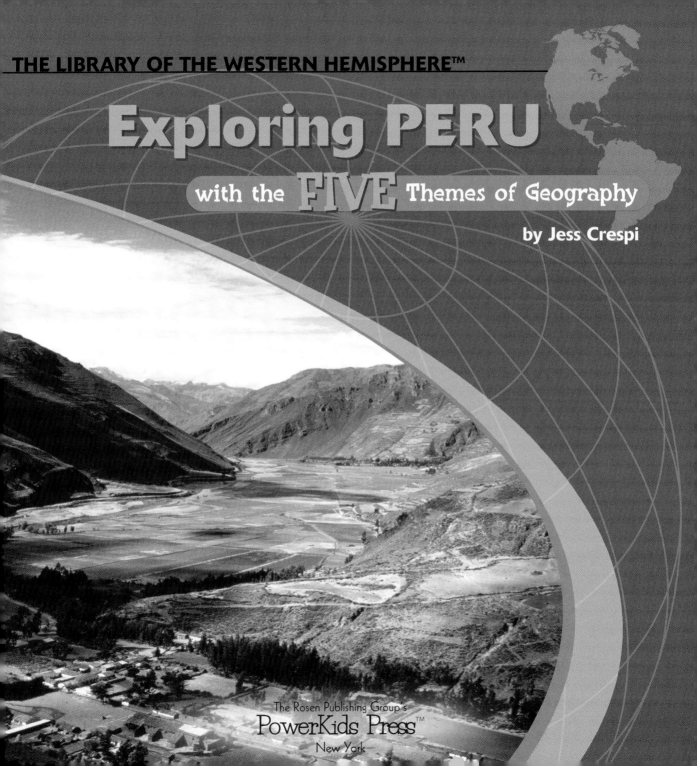

Exploring PERU

with the FIVE Themes of Geography

by Jess Crespi

The Rosen Publishing Group's
PowerKids Press™
New York

Published in 2005 by The Rosen Publishing Group, Inc.
29 East 21st Street, New York, NY 10010

First Edition

Editor: Geeta Sobha
Book Design: Michelle Innes

Photo Credits: Cover, p. 1 © James Strachan/Getty Images; p. 9 © Kevin Schafer/Getty Images;
pp. 9 (Manu Park), 15 © Kevin Schafer/Corbis; p. 10 © Hubert Stadler/Corbis; p. 10 (Anaconda)
© Brian Kenney/Getty Images; p. 10 (macaws) © Grant Faint/Getty Images; p. 12 © Adrian
Lyon/Getty Images; p. 12 (Nazca Rines) © Andrea Pistolesi/Getty Images; p. 12 (church) © Danny
Lehman/Corbis; p. 15 (farms) © Robert Frerck/Getty Images; p. 16 © Collart Herve/Corbis Sygma;
p. 16 (logging factory) © Alison Wright; pp. 19, 21 (volcano) © Yann Arthus-Bertrand/Corbis; p. 19
(highway) © James Sparshatt/Corbis

Library of Congress Cataloging-in-Publication Data

Crespi, Jess.
    Exploring Peru with the five themes of geography / by Jess Crespi.— 1st ed.
    p. cm. — (Library of the Western Hemisphere)
    Includes index.
    ISBN 1-4042-2676-1 (lib. bdg.) — ISBN 0-8239-4636-3 (pbk.)
    1. Peru—Geography—Juvenile literature. I. Title. II. Series.

F3410.4.C74 2005
918.5—dc22

                                                        2004003118

Manufactured in the United States of America

Contents

The Five Themes of Geography 4

1 Location 6

2 Place 8

3 Human-Environment Interaction 14

4 Movement 18

5 Regions 20

Fact Zone 22

Glossary 23

Index 24

Web Sites 24

The FIVE Themes of Geography

Geography is the study of Earth, including its people, resources, climate, and physical features. To study a particular country or area, such as Peru, we use the five themes of geography: location, place, human-environment interaction, movement, and regions. By using these themes, we can organize and understand important information about the geography of places throughout the world. Let's use the five themes to learn about Peru.

1 Location

Where is Peru?

Peru's position can be defined by using its absolute, or exact, location. Absolute location tells exactly where a place is in the world. The imaginary lines of longitude and latitude are used to define absolute location.

Peru can also be found by using its relative, or general, location. Relative location describes where a place is by showing other places near it. Also, relative location can be described by using the cardinal directions of east, west, north, and south.

2 Place

What is Peru like?

To really know Peru, we must study its physical and human features. The physical features include landforms, bodies of water, climate, natural resources, and plant and animal life. The human features are things, such as cities, buildings, government, and traditions, that have been created by people.

3 Human-Environment Interaction

How do the people and the environment of Peru affect each other?

Human-environment interaction explains how people rely on the environment. It also explains how people adapt to the environment. Lastly, it explains how the people have changed their environment to better suit their needs.

4 Movement

How do people, goods, and ideas get from place to place in Peru?

This theme explains how people, products, and ideas move around the country. It can also show how they move from Peru to other places.

5 Regions

What does Peru have in common with other places around the world? What features do places within Peru share to make them part of a region?

Places are grouped into regions by features that they share. We will study features that Peru shares with other areas, making it part of certain geographic and cultural regions. We'll also look at political and physical regions within Peru.

Peru's absolute location is 10° south and 76° west. Peru's relative location can be defined by looking at the places that surround it. Peru is bordered by Ecuador and Colombia on the north. Brazil and Bolivia are on Peru's eastern border. Chile lies to the south, and the Pacific Ocean is along Peru's west coast. Peru is located in western South America.

Where in the World?

Absolute location is the point where the lines of longitude and latitude meet.

Longitude tells a place's position in degrees east or west of the prime meridian, a line that runs through Greenwich, London.

Latitude tells a place's position in degrees north or south of the equator, the imaginary line that goes around the middle of the earth.

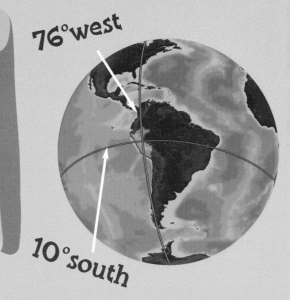

76°west

10°south

Physical Features

Peru has three main geographic regions: the costa, the sierra, and the selva. The costa is the desert coastal area that runs from north to south. Though some rivers run through the costa, many dry out before reaching the coast. The northern part of the costa is flatland, while the south is mountainous. The climate in the west of the costa is mostly dry and cool. The east is warm and humid.

The sierra region is made up of the Andes Mountains. The highest peaks can be found in the central mountain ranges. Peru's tallest mountain, Mount Huascarán, is located in the Andes. The southern ranges are made up of volcanoes. Depending on the season, temperatures are from about 20° to 70°F (-7° to 21°C).

Manu National Park in the selva is home to over 1,000 types of birds.

Lake Titicaca lies on the border of Peru and Bolivia.

Peru's largest animal, the anaconda, lives in the selva. It is a giant snake that can grow up to 33 feet (10 meters) long.

The puya raimondii tree takes nearly 100 years to grow to its full size of 30 feet (9 m). It is found in the Andes Mountains.

Scarlet macaws live in the rain forests of the selva.

The selva, in eastern Peru, makes up the largest area of the country. It is part of the Amazon rain forest. The weather in the selva is hot and humid. Some areas get as much as 150 inches (381 centimeters) of rain per year.

Many types of animals live in Peru. Albatrosses and terns, both of which are birds, as well as lizards and scorpions make their homes in the costa. Sea lions also live in the costa. Llamas, alpacas, chinchillas, and flamingos live in the sierra. Jaguars, cougars, anteaters, and parrots can be found in the selva. Anchovy, sole, flounder, and tuna are among the fishes found in Peru's ocean waters.

Mesquite trees and a mix of grasses grow in the costa. Mahogany, cedar, and cinchona trees grow in the selva. Sarsaparilla and vanilla plants also grow there. Sierra plant life includes cactus and eucalyptus plants.

La Compania de Jesus church is in Cuzco. It was built on top of an Incan building by the Spanish.

The Nazca Lines can be found in the city of Nazca. They were made over 2,000 years ago by ancient Nazca people.

The remains of Incan architecture can be seen in Machu Picchu in the Andes.

Human Features

Most of Peru's large cities are in the costa. Over 70 percent of the people live in cities, especially Lima and Callao. Almost half of Peru's population is Native American. About one-third are mestizos. Mestizos are descended from both Spanish and Native American peoples.

Peru's culture is influenced by both Native American and Spanish peoples. There are three official languages in Peru: Spanish, Aymará, and Quechua. The latter two are languages of the Incas, who ruled Peru before Spain. Ancient Incan architecture has been blended with Spanish styles in the city of Cuzco. In Lima, both modern and Spanish colonial-style buildings can be seen.

Peru's form of government is a constitutional republic. The government is led by a president, who is elected by the people for a five-year term.

Peruvians take advantage of the natural resources of their country. The most important resource is Peru's land. Farming is important to Peru's economy. The costa is the most farmed area in Peru. Farmers grow sugarcane, cotton, rice, grapes, and vegetables. Because the costa gets very little rain, Peruvians have created an irrigation system to get water to crops.

Mining is also important in Peru. Peru is one of the world's most important sources of copper, silver, lead, and zinc. Petroleum and natural gas are produced in great amounts.

Water is an important resource for two reasons: hydroelectric power and fishing. Eighty-five percent of Peru uses hydroelectric power. Also, Peru has one of the largest fishing industries in the world. Peru exports anchovies and fish meal.

Small farms in the sierra region produce crops for local use.

Iquitos is the largest city in the selva. It is the center of Peru's rubber, oil, and logging industries.

Lumber from trees such as balsa is produced in Peru's logging factories.

Mining for iron can pollute waterways with toxins.

The growth of industries such as logging and petroleum has had both positive and negative effects on Peru. Many jobs have been created, along with roads and housing. However, this has caused the clearing of forested land. Both wildlife and native tribes living in these areas have had to move.

Many industries are located around the major cities, such as Lima. This has resulted in air pollution and water pollution of rivers and coastal waters.

Every few years, Peru is faced with an unusual change in the weather known as El Niño. Warm ocean currents flow south from the equator. This kills many of the fish that live in the cold waters along Peru's coast. People who depend on the fishing industry are affected by this loss. El Niño also causes storms, with heavy rains, floods, and mudslides. El Niño has been responsible for many deaths in Peru.

4 Movement

The Andes Mountains make travel from east to west difficult. The Pan-American Highway, which connects most of South America, runs north to south through eastern Peru. Peruvians use cars, buses, or trucks to move around.

Goods are shipped to and from Peru through ports along the Pacific coast. Callao is the largest port in the country. Lake Titicaca and the Amazon River are important waterways for movement in Peru. Airplanes not only move people in and out of Peru, but they are also important for reaching places deep in the forest areas.

News and ideas move across Peru in many ways. Peru has about 13 television stations and over 900 radio stations. Newspapers include *El Comercio* and *La República*, both of which are published in Lima. Writers, such as Mario Vargas Llosa, are recognized all over the world.

The port in Callao is important to Peru's fishing industry.

There are 45,298 miles (72,900 kilometers) of highways in Peru. However, only 9,331 miles (15,017 km) are paved.

Regions

Peru is part of both cultural and geographic regions. Peru is part of the cultural region known as Latin America, where most people speak a Romance language, such as Spanish, French, or Portuguese. Latin America is made up of countries in the Western Hemisphere south of the United States, including the West Indies.

Peru is within the geographical region called the Ring of Fire. This is an area that stretches around the Pacific Ocean. Many earthquakes and volcanoes occur in this region.

Peru is divided into three physical regions: the costa, the sierra, and the selva. It is also divided into political regions. There are 24 departments and one constitutional province. Each department has a local government.

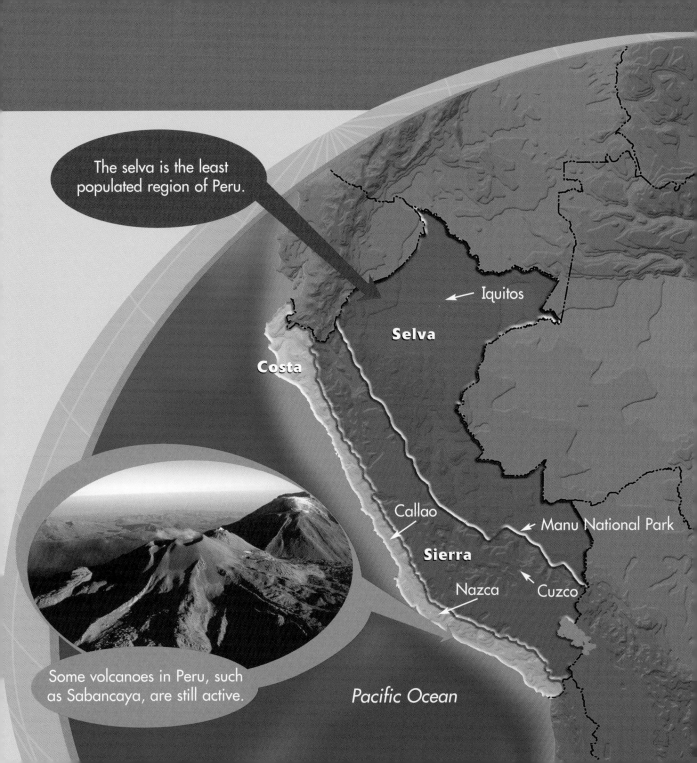

The selva is the least populated region of Peru.

Some volcanoes in Peru, such as Sabancaya, are still active.

Selva

Costa

Iquitos

Callao

Sierra

Manu National Park

Nazca

Cuzco

Pacific Ocean

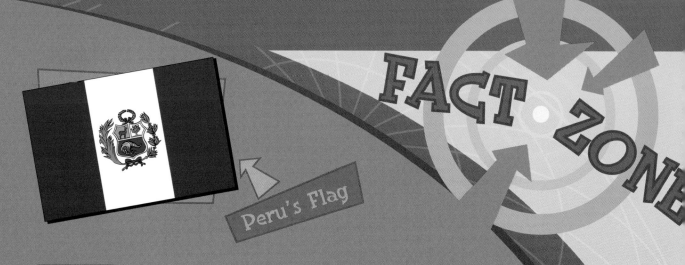

Peru's Flag

Population (2003) 28,409,897

Languages Spanish, Quechua, and Aymará

Absolute location 10° south, 76° west

Capital city Lima

Area 496,226 square miles (1,285,220 square kilometers)

Highest point Mount Huascarán 22,205 feet (6,768 meters)

Lowest point Pacific Ocean zero feet

Land boundaries Bolivia, Brazil, Chile, Colombia, and Ecuador

Natural resources copper, silver, gold, petroleum, timber, fish, iron ore, coal, phosphate, potash, hydropower, and natural gas

Agricultural products coffee, cotton, sugarcane, rice, wheat, potatoes, corn, plantains, poultry, beef, dairy products, wool, and fish

Major exports fish and fish products, gold, copper, zinc, crude petroleum and byproducts, lead, coffee, sugar, and cotton

Major imports machinery, transportation equipment, foodstuffs, petroleum, iron, steel, chemicals, and pharmaceuticals

Glossary

architecture (AR-ki-tek-chur) The style in which buildings are designed.

culture (KUHL-chur) The way of life, ideas, customs, and traditions shared by a group of people.

hemisphere (HEM-uhss-fihr) One half of the earth.

hydroelectric power (hye-droh-i-LEK-trik POU-ur) Water power that is used to turn a generator to produce electricity.

interaction (in-tur-AK-shuhn) The action between people, groups, or things.

irrigation (ihr-uh-GAY-shuhn) When water is applied to crops by using channels and pipes.

region (REE-juhn) An area or a district.

resource (ri-SORSS) Something that is valuable or useful to a place or person.

volcano (vol-KA-noh) A mountain with an opening through which steam, ashes, and lava are sometimes forced out.

Index

A
Amazon rain forest, 11
Amazon River, 18
Andes Mountains, 8, 18
animals, 11

B
Bolivia, 6
Brazil, 6

C
Chile, 6
Colombia, 6
constitutional republic, 13
costa, 8, 11, 13, 14, 20

E
Ecuador, 6
El Niño, 17

F
farming, 14
fishing, 14

G
government, 13, 20

I
Incas, 13
industry, 14, 17
irrigation system, 14

L
Lake Titicaca, 18
languages, 13
Latin America, 20
Lima, 13, 17, 18

M
mestizos, 13
mining, 14
Mount Huascarán, 8

P
Pacific Ocean, 6, 20
Pan-American Highway, 18
pollution, 17
port, 18

R
resource, 4, 5, 14
Ring of Fire, 20

S
selva, 8, 11, 20
sierra, 8, 11, 20
South America, 6, 18

T
travel, 18
trees, 11

V
volcanoes, 8, 20

Web Sites

Due to the changing nature of Internet links, PowerKids Press has developed an on-line list of Web sites related to the subject of this book. This site is updated regularly. Please use this link to access the list:
http://www.powerkidslinks.com/lwh/peru